Winter's Promise

Winter's Promise

KEN GIRE

HARVEST HOUSE PUBLISHERS
EUGENE, OREGON

Cover by Garborg Design Works, Savage, Minnesota
Cover photo © Bigstock / DTPhoto
Interior photos by Janet Potter

Published in association with the literary agency of WordServe Literary Group, Ltd., 10152 S. Knoll Circle, Highlands Ranch, CO 80130

Material in this book is adapted from other books by Ken Gire. See the endnotes for more information.

WINTER'S PROMISE

Copyright © 2013 by Ken Gire
Published by Harvest House Publishers
Eugene, Oregon 97402
www.harvesthousepublishers.com

ISBN 978-0-7369-5649-9 (hardcover)
ISBN 978-0-7369-5650-5 (eBook)

Printed in China

13 14 15 16 17 18 19 20 21 22 /RDS-JH / 10 9 8 7 6 5 4 3 2 1

Contents

Introduction

This book includes various metaphors that I have used in other books to capture some aspects of our relationship with God. Moments of revelation are described as windows of the soul, moments of intimacy are compared to a dance, moments of suffering are referred to as the weathering grace of God, and moments when God is silent are described as being on the North Face of God, an image from Mount Everest.

The images are ways of saying that our relationship with God goes through different seasons. Each season has its challenges, its difficulties—spring's harrowing and furrowing, summer's scorching heat, autumn's changing and dying, winter's cold and death.

Each season also has its beauties and promise—spring's new life and promise, summer's busy fun, autumn's gentle whispered beauty, winter's secret joy and hope.

In the winter season, God's silence seems to resound across the lonely snow-swept plains. The long evenings, filled with thinking, sometimes regretting; the short days, almost not long enough to complete anything of value. It is a time of waiting, of reflecting, and of hoping. Yet through it all, a promise lies in the seed of new life, waiting to spring up and fill the earth with beauty in God's perfect time.

Chapter One

A Season's Silence

In our noisy world, extended periods
of silence can make us feel uncomfortable.
But if we let ourselves grow accustomed
to the stillness, might we learn to
hear a different kind of sound?

The Colors of Silence

The silence of winter falls like a blanket, canvassing the landscape under its spell. You almost feel that if you speak a decibel too loud, the spell will be broken. So the days carry on in silence.

Sometimes a gray silence, a lifeless shroud, under which lies the remnants of what was a vibrant life.

Sometimes a white silence, a soft blanket, under which all life sleeps.

The silence has lasted so long, it seems, that straining to catch even the memory of the sound of joy is too far.

The song of a robin in spring. The low cooing of a dove in summer. The geese overhead in fall.

A baby's laughter in spring. Children joyfully shouting in summer. Family giving thanks in the autumn.

Are the sounds hidden here, somewhere beneath the silent gray and white? Can they be searched out?

Discovered?

Recovered?

Times of silence can be treasured. A time to recall blessed memories. A time to plan new ones. A time to hear, perhaps not song, perhaps not even laughter, but the whisper upon the heart.

The whisper that says, *It is well, for I am with you.*

God's Voice in the Silence

Though it is his nature to speak, sometimes God is silent. And maybe the purpose of his silence is to give resonance to the words he has already spoken to you or to me. Or maybe he is simply waiting for us to trust and obey what he has already revealed to us before he reveals anything else.

The silence of God can be a devastating thing. But maybe, even through his silence, God is saying something, just as through our silence in a conversation we too are saying something.

Maybe the silence is saying, "I'm giving your words my full attention, and I want to hear everything you have to say before I respond."

Maybe the silence is saying that now is not the appropriate time to say anything. Maybe the silence means, "What I have to say, if I said it now, wouldn't be understood…or received… or fully appreciated."

Maybe the silence means, "I'm waiting for you to say something else before I speak. I want you to come to some conclusions on your own instead of me spelling it out for you."

Or maybe the silence means, "I just want so much for you

to hear that I'm using the silence to heighten your attention so that when I do speak, you will hear every word."

Take some time to examine the silence of God in your own experience. Try to hear some echo of God's voice in those silences.[1]

Listening with the Soul

God stretched out the heavens, stippling the night with impressionistic stars. He set the sun to the rhythm of the day, the moon to the rhythm of the month, the seasons to the rhythm of the year. He formed a likeness of himself from a lump of clay and into it breathed life. He crafted a counterpart to complete the likeness, joining the two halves and placing them center stage in his creation, where there was a temptation and a fall, a great loss and a great hiding. God searched for the hiding couple, reaching to pick them up, dust them off, draw them near. After them, he searched for their children and for their children's children.

Shaped from something of earth and something of heaven, we were torn between two worlds. A part of us wanted to hide. A part of us wanted to search. With half-remembered words still legible in our hearts and faintly sketched images still visible in our souls, some of us stepped out of hiding and started our search.

We reach for God in many ways. Through our sculptures and our Scriptures. Through our pictures and our prayers. Through our writing and our worship. And through them he reaches for us.

His search begins with something said. Ours begins with something heard. His begins with something shown. Ours, with something seen. Our search for God and his search for us meet at windows in our everyday experience.

We must learn to look with more than just our eyes and listen with more than just our ears, for the sounds are sometimes faint and the sights sometimes far away. We must be aware, at all times and in all places, because windows of the soul are everywhere, and at any time we may find one. Or one may find us. Though we will hardly know it unless we are searching for him who for so long has been searching for us. [2]

Listening Underneath Creation

One day I took a walk up the mountains behind my office, and I sat on the bank of the Palmer Lake Reservoir, which was just beginning to thaw. The entire lake was covered with ice except for the six-inch margin closest to shore. I was looking in the clear water to the pebbles a few inches below the surface when I caught a reflection of the sun in its rippling surface.

The light was broken into a prism of colors, and behind the prism was a veil of clouds, and behind the clouds, the sun. I looked up to see this beautiful image in the sky, but even through the clouds, even through the filter of the earth's atmosphere, even through a distance of ninety-three million miles, my eyes couldn't take in the sun without having to shield them with my hand.

We cannot look at the sun in its noonday glory. Neither can we see God in his glory. And so he comes to us in ways that our senses can take him in without injury, which is always less than he is. And this helped me understand why God speaks to us in the ways he sometimes does.

In *A River Runs Through It*, Norman Maclean's father, a Presbyterian minister, is sitting on the bank of the river, reading the Gospel of John while his sons are fishing. When Norman comes over to where he is sitting, the father pensively remarks: "In the part I was reading, it says the Word was in the beginning...I used to think water was first, but if you listen carefully you will hear that the words are underneath the water."

Underneath the creation are the words of life, "Let there be...and there was."

God's words are underneath everything. And if you listen carefully, you will hear them. [3]

Choosing to Sit Still

The vacation Anne Morrow Lindbergh once took on an East Coast beach, which she chronicled in her book *Gift from the Sea*, offers an excellent model for reflective living. It is full of wit and wisdom and rich reflections about life.

> I begin to understand why the saints were rarely married women. I am convinced it has nothing inherently to do, as I once supposed, with chastity or children. It has to do primarily with distractions. The bearing, rearing, feeding and educating of children; the running of a house with its thousand details; human relationships with their myriad pulls—woman's normal occupations in general run counter to creative life, or contemplative life, or saintly life.

How do we remain whole in the midst of the distractions of life? It's a question we all wrestle with. But for Christians the question goes deeper. In the midst of the distractions of life, how do we remain wholly devoted to Christ?

We do what Mary did.

We make a choice to sit at Christ's feet. That is where the

many things we are involved in are brought into submission to the one thing that is necessary (Luke 10:38-42).

To Christ's feet we bring the many things in our lives for his scrutiny. There we submit to him our plans, our goals, our dreams, our work, our opportunities, our schedules…and we ask him, "Which ones, Lord? Which things would you want me to do? In which activities can I serve you best? What work would be the best stewardship of the gifts you have entrusted to me? What should I say yes to, Lord? And to what should I say no?"

Then we wait for his answer, which often doesn't come right away, but in his own time and in his own way. The farther we are from his feet, the harder it will be to hear that answer. In a busy kitchen, it is almost impossible.

The choice to get busy or to sit still, to work in the kitchen or to wait at Christ's feet, is essentially a decision of whether to submit the details of our lives to his lordship. Deciding to submit them simplifies our lives because it makes us accountable to one Master instead of to a pantheon of competing ones. [4]

The Still Point in the Dance

Except for the point, the still point,
there would be no dance, and
there is only the dance.

T.S. ELIOT

Love changes us in ways that law cannot. Spiritual forma-
tion, the process of being changed into the image of
Christ, doesn't happen by following disciplines. It happens by
falling in love. When we fall in love with Jesus, all the other
loves in our lives fall into place. And those that once com-
peted with Christ now subordinate themselves to him. Everything in our lives finds its proper value once we have properly
valued him.

We take time for what we value. And we behold what we
love. It is not the duty of beholding that changes us, though,
but rather the beauty of the one we behold. When Christ at
last appears, we will behold him in all his beauty and for all
eternity. And we will be like him, John says, because we will
see him for the first time as he really is (see 1 John 3:2).

One day we *will* be transformed. And it will be a face that
transforms us. That face transforms us here on this earth as
well, though here we see it through a glass darkly, often distort-
edly, and only fleetingly (see 1 Corinthians 13:12).

That is why busyness is lethal—it keeps us from beholding

the face of Jesus. And that is why stillness is essential—to get the best possible look at his face for the longest possible time.

Beholding Christ's face is the still point of the dance, around which all our activity should revolve.

If that is not the still point in our lives, there is no dance.

There is only movement. [5]

Listening in the Stillness

My soul waits in silence for God only;
From Him is my salvation.

PSALM 62:1

Poets know the importance of this kind of stillness. They know that if they are still enough, long enough, the art they are working on will speak to them, tell them what it wants to be and what it needs from them to become it. All artists know this whether they work with paint or clay, words or musical notes.

Michelangelo knew how to be still before the stone and listen to the David within it. Strauss knew how to be still before the Danube and listen to the waltz that was eddying about in its waters. Monet knew how to be still before the pond and listen to the lilies sunning on its surface.

What we are asking to listen to is the voice of the Great Artist himself, who will one day bring, out of the upheavals in this world, a new heaven and a new earth. And who is in the process of bringing, out of the upheavals in our lives, a new heaven and new earth within us as well.

Our culture knows little of this kind of listening. That is true of our religious culture as well, as A.W. Tozer explains in his book *The Pursuit of God.*

Religion has accepted the monstrous heresy that noise, size, activity and bluster make a man dear to God. But we may take heart. To a people caught in the tempest of the last great conflict God says, "Be still, and know that I am God," and still He says it, as if He means to tell us that our strength and safety lie not in noise but in silence.[6]

An Expression of Deepest Longing

Between heaven and earth lies the firmament of our prayers. In one sense, the firmament is ethereal as air. In another sense, it is substantial as atmosphere. In a sense, it is a mere wisp of who we are. In another sense, it is rich with the elements of life, gritty with the dust of our humanity.

Within this ever-changing sky funnels a maelstrom of faith and doubt. Turbulent at times with gales of emotion. Wild and windswept and full of fury. A swirling vortex of questions, arguments, and confusion.

But that is not all there is to the weather of the heart.

There are calm days too. Serene as a sunset. A tinting of thankfulness on the horizon. A billowing of praise. And, thank God, for most of us, there are more blue skies than storms.

Some prayers have been sighed into the heat of day. Others have been shivered into the cold loneliness of night. Together, they make up the atmosphere.

And together they celebrate an intimate God.

A God who listened and spoke, cleaving all of human history with a word.

Immanuel.

God with us.

Prayer is, I think, an expression of our deepest longing. Unspoken syllables tearfully ascending an expansive sky.

Snowflaking into a word. Something beautiful from heaven descending to earth.

Glistening with grace and truth. Settling on our shoulders. Touching us with wonder. And love. And hope.

Immanuel.

Perhaps it is more than a name.

Perhaps in the firmament between heaven and earth
  it is both a prayer
    and an answer to prayer. [7]

A Question in the Stillness

As we pull the covers to our chins at night and settle into our pillows, one question should bring our day into the presence of God for his scrutiny. Did the life I lived today please you, God?

How many things do we have to check off our to-do list before we can say yes to a question like that? How many questions do we have to count before we can be done with them all and drop off to sleep?

Only one.

Have I loved well?

St. John of the Cross once said that "at the evening of our day we shall be judged by our loving." As we look back over our day, what we have done is not as important as how we have done it. Better to do little with much love than much with little love. For without love, whatever we do will be dismissed with a judicial wave of heaven's hand as just so many trivial pursuits (1 Corinthians 13:1-3).

So it's the end of the day, and each of us is lying in bed, reflecting. Have I loved well? Has love been the beating heart pulsing through all my activities? Can it be heard in all my conversations? Seen in my eyes? Felt when other people are in my presence? Was the truth I spoke today spoken in love?

Were the decisions I made today based on love? Were my reactions? My devotions?

Have I loved well?

If we can answer yes to that question, it is enough.

It may not be enough for our employer. It may not be enough for our fellow workers. It may not be enough for all the carpools and committees and other things on our calendars.

It may not even be enough for us.

But it is enough for God.

And that should make it enough for us. [8]

A Sound in the Stillness

All the things that have ever deeply possessed your soul have been but hints—tantalizing glimpses, promises never quite fulfilled, echoes that died away just as they caught your ear. But if it should really become manifest—if there ever came an echo that did not die away but swelled into the sound itself—you would know it. Beyond all possibility of doubt you would say, "Here at last is the thing I was made for."

When we live our lives with an inner stillness, the way a weaned child rests against its mother, we get a sense not only of oneness with the Father but a certainty of his purpose for our lives.

When we know our gifting, our calling, that thing we were made for, we can serve God more effectively because there is less wasted motion to our activity. Love, joy, and peace are just some of the fruit.

Love comes while we rest against our Father's chest.

Joy comes when we catch the rhythms of his heart.

Peace comes when we live in harmony with those rhythms.

Within the closeness and warmth of that relationship, we gain the certainty that we are doing the very thing he would have us do with our lives. Whether that thing is motherhood or sainthood, God only knows. But if we crawl onto his lap, lay our head against his chest, and listen…he will tell us. [9]

A Soft Voice in the Routine

It is hardest to hear God in the drone of our daily routine. It seems not to matter much if the gears of that routine grind indoors or outdoors, in an office or a home, in a classroom or a church room.

Each of those places seems to have its own set of clockwork rhythms. Whether set to the minute or the hour or the setting of the sun, each has its own way of ordering our steps and occupying our thoughts.

Which makes it difficult to hear.

Like Martha, maybe we are too distracted by our work to hear.

Like the man who passed up the dinner invitation because he had business to attend to, maybe we are too driven by our work to hear.

Whether it's the drivenness of work or the distractions created by the work, the workplace is often the least conducive place for the wisdom of God to be heard. Yet the voice of wisdom calls from the teeming center of such a place, Solomon says (Proverbs 1:20-21; 8:1-3). And lest we should forget…

It was to shepherds at work in their fields that the message from heaven came.

It was to fishermen cleaning their nets that the call to become disciples came.

It was to soldiers on a Friday shift that the word of forgiveness came.

I wonder. How many of the soldiers who showed up for work that day heard that word? Only one that we know of. A centurion. Assigned to the dirty work of overseeing the execution of three common criminals. All day long the centurion went about the routine of his work, waiting for them to die. Watching, as one by one they did. Listening, as they gasped their last words.

As he waited there, what he saw and heard from one of them made him realize that it was no common criminal who died on one of those crosses.

"Truly this man was the Son of God!"

The other soldiers put in their time and were paid their day's wages.

One of them even took home a bonus—a garment he was lucky enough to win.

But only the centurion, only the centurion heard
    what God had spoken
        during that routine workday
            on that Friday afternoon shift. [10]

The Call to Be Still

"Cease striving and know that I am God" (Psalm 46:10). The call to be still, to stand silent, to cease striving, comes in the context of a life in chaos. A life surrounded by landslides, tidal waves, and earthquakes. Whether the chaos is environmental, political, relational, emotional, or simply organizational, there is a river, the psalmist tells us, that flows from the throne of God. A river that remains clear and refreshing, undisturbed by the upheavals. A river whose streams bring gladness. The gladness we can have in the midst of turbulent times, the peace that flows like a river, is the nearness of our God.

"The Lord of hosts is with us," the psalmist assures us.

"The God of Jacob is our stronghold."

He is with us when our world caves in around us.

When the marriage others looked up to slips into the heart of the sea. When once-calm relationships now roar and foam. When the once-stable mountain of financial security now quakes.

He is "our refuge and strength."

"A very present help in trouble."

We will never know it, though, unless we cease striving and still our hearts. [11]

Waiting in the Silence

The silences are not to be feared. For it is in the silences that God most often speaks.

If that is true, it stands to reason that we increase our odds of hearing what he has to say if we still our souls, calm our hearts, quiet the yammering of our own inner voices. And wait.

This waiting silence is a biblical pattern for hearing God. Eli told Samuel how to hear God's voice, which at first was unfamiliar to the young boy, when the priest counseled him to call out into the night with the words, "Speak, LORD, for Your servant is listening" (1 Samuel 3:9). David tried to bring about this receptive stillness within himself when he said, "My soul, wait in silence for God only" (Psalm 62:5). And Jeremiah advised the person seeking God, "It is good that he waits silently for the salvation of the Lord" (Lamentations 3:26).

But though the pattern is a biblical one, it is by no means a natural one. Our natural tendencies are restive, not reflective.

Prayer is most often thought of as a time for us to speak with God. But it is also, I think, a time for God to speak with us. Sometimes he speaks with articulate clarity. Other times, with groaning too deep for words, speaking from his Spirit to ours in the form of some inner conviction. He may not respond immediately. He may answer later in the day or later in life, for his sense of urgency is different from ours.

There are moments in prayer, however, when God does speak. As in any conversation, though, unless we pause to listen, we're likely to miss it. As you take time to pray, try talking less and listening more. It is of course possible you won't hear anything. But if you're not listening, it's certain you won't. [12]

CHAPTER TWO

A Season's Waiting

Why is waiting sometimes so difficult?
Perhaps because our work is done
for a time and we can do little else to
reach our desired end…but trust.

Questions in the Night

In winter, it seems that before the sun has had a chance to rise in all its fullness, bestowing its golden glory, it is already descending the sky. Before the landscape has had the opportunity to bathe in the glow, the sun has dissolved into a tinge of dusty rose and indigo. By the next glance, even the shadows have sought refuge from the fast approaching evening.

The sky is dark.

There is nothing to do but wait for the sun to rise again.

And wait.

And wait.

The evenings are long. The nights longer. The questions inevitably start to rise.

What am I waiting for? Is it worth this long wait? Will I make it through the night?

Only time will tell. Yet for the moment, there is no choice but to wait.

There is a time for every purpose under heaven. And at the times of waiting, perhaps more is happening than meets the eye.

The work of patience.

And drawing near to him who holds time within his hands, and us within his heart.

Waiting for Dawn

Everyone's night on the mountain is different, both in degree and in duration.

So is everyone's dawn.

A scene in J.R.R. Tolkien's book *The Two Towers* describes Middle-earth in one of its darkest nights. After the forces of good, led by Aragorn, retreat to Helms Deep, the forces of evil gather outside the fortress walls. The odds against Aragorn and his men are overwhelming. Although Gandalf has promised help from the east at the first light of dawn, there is no sign of him. As far as the eye can see, there is only darkness and the sea of enemy forces.

Aragorn looked at the pale stars, and at the moon, now sloping behind the western hills that enclosed the valley. "This is a night as long as years," he said. "How long will the day tarry?"

"Dawn is not far off," said Gamling, who had now climbed up beside him. "But dawn will not help us, I fear."

"Yet dawn is ever the hope of men," said Aragorn.

Although everyone's dark night is different, everyone's way out of the darkness is the same. The only way out of the darkness of night is the coming of the dawn, which is the hope of all who have faced their worst fears in the night.

The dawn that ends your night may be a full-orbed miracle

or simply a ray of hope. It may be a revelation from heaven that illuminates your suffering or simply a graying of the horizon that allows you enough light to move on with your life.

Though it may not be the dawn we have been waiting for, it is the dawn God has been waiting for.

> *Dear Lord,*
>
> *Help me to understand that somewhere on the mountain, a dark night will come upon my soul.*
>
> *Help me to realize how dangerous the darkness is.*
>
> *One misstep, and I could lose everything: my marriage, my family, my reputation, my faith, even my life.*
>
> *Help me make it through the night, Lord.*
>
> *Give me patience to wait for the dawn and to realize that even in the darkness you are at work, breaking down the husk around the seed of my understanding and bringing life, new and emerging life that will have its day in the sun and share in the companionship of all living things. [1]*

How Will We Wait?

Weeping may last through the night," the psalmist writes, "but joy comes with the morning" (Psalm 30:5).

How do we get to the morning, to the sunshine, to the joy? There is only one way.

By waiting for it. We can't hurry the dawn, no matter how anxiously we pace the floor or how impatiently we watch the clock. And so the question is not, do we wait or not wait? The question is, *how* will we wait?

One of the many things nature teaches us is how to wait. All living things wait through the chill of night for the dawn. And they wait through the cold of March for the spring. That is the cycle of physical life: the fragile stem straightening into the light…the seed…the dark…the long wait…and the light again.

That is also the cycle of spiritual life.

As much as we would like it to be different, there is no eternal sunshine of the soul, no endless spring. Understanding that makes enduring the darkness easier.

And as much as it may feel like it at the time, there is no eternal night either, no endless winter. Understanding that makes waiting for the dawn easier.

And as we wait, we pray.

Our prayers may not hurry the sun, but they will heighten our awareness of what is happening in the darkness. Even in the dark of night and the cold of March, God is at work, breaking through the husk around our hearts and bringing life from under dead leaves. [2]

Blessed Company in the Waiting

In some way, Jesus needs our love. In Revelation 3:20, Jesus says: "Behold, I stand at the door and knock; if anyone hears My voice and opens the door, I will come in to him, and will dine with him, and he with Me."

That time together is for both of us. I will dine with him, Jesus said, and he with me. It is a shared meal, not a solitary one. If we don't show up for the meal, he goes away hungry. There is an emptiness in him that only you can fill. And one that only I can fill. Realizing that, I suddenly feel guilty for all the times he has hungered for my company and I wasn't there to give it. But then I look into his eyes and I realize something else.

He doesn't want us to feel guilty.

He wants us to feel in love.

He *needs* us to feel in love.

Jesus has gone ahead of us to prepare a place for us, but if we don't show up, there will be no honeymoon. A wedding feast has been prepared for us too, but if we don't come, there will be no celebration. He can love us without our loving him back, but if we don't love him back, his joy is not made full. And in that sense, he needs our love.

One resplendent day, his love for us and ours for him will be celebrated in heaven. A feast, we are told, awaits us there.

Meanwhile, here on earth, Jesus shares with us a table set for two.

There are words he longs to say to you and to me. And words he longs to hear from us. This is our food and our drink, our daily bread and cup of wine.

It is also his. [3]

Presence in the Darkness

Buddhists see mountains as peaks of consciousness where pure understanding can be found. That is why caves around Everest are full of hermits seeking ultimate enlightenment. Christians look at the world differently. For us, pure understanding is found not in nature but in the God of nature. So we look not to the mountains for our help but to the God who created them. As the psalmist reminds us...

> I look up to the mountains—
> does my help come from there?
> My help comes from the Lord,
> who made heaven and earth! (Psalm 121:1-2)

Sometimes, though, that help is hard to see. As C.S. Lewis explains, God is in his creation in much the same way that Shakespeare is in his plays. The playwright cannot be found in any one scene, one character, or one line of dialogue. Yet at the same time, he is everywhere—in every scene, every character, every line of dialogue. So it is on the North Face of God. *Where is he?* we wonder. We look around us, and he is nowhere to be found. And then, when we look with the right eyes, we see traces of him everywhere.

He was there in the strength we had within us to make the climb.

He was there in the faith it took to cross the shaky footbridge that stretched over the crevasse of abysmal circumstances.

He was there in the partner who was roped to us, steadying us as we went.

He was there in the climbing team that accompanied us, bringing different people into our lives at different times to make sure we had the help we needed.

He was there in the dawn to make sure the darkness didn't overwhelm us.

He was there every step of the way, though not always in the ways we expected.

Dear Lord,

Help me to understand that I am part of a divine work that has been millennia in the making.

Though my place may be small, it is significant; though fragmentary, it is full of meaning.

I pray that whatever suffering comes to me in this life would, through your gentle hand, become part of a mosaic that helps to tell a beautiful story of redemption.

Grant me the grace to reach a summit of understanding about my circumstances. And if not a summit, at least a ledge where I can come to peace with them, and with the peace…find rest. [4]

Dormant in the Soil

There is a battle, a war, and the casualties could be our hearts and souls. The Christian life is about passion. Passion for God and passion for people in need. These are the words and ideas that when enfleshed can change the world. These are the things we live for.

But those things can easily get lost. One way is by detaching them from the object of our love. When we do that, all we're left with are actions that only resemble love. Empty, impersonal acts. Like sex without love. And when sex is detached from love, it is reduced to technique. People may write handbooks on it, but not poetry.

All of us at some time or another have been guilty of approaching Scripture that way. Detaching it from the source of its love. Dissecting it in order to study it.

We study it as a handbook of principles when we should see it as poetry.

We study it as a treatise on theology when we should see it as beauty.

We study it as a record of biblical history when we should see it as romance.

We study it as a code of conduct when we should see it as love.

The Bible is, first and foremost, a love letter. The words

in that letter are like seeds that fall into the soil of our hearts. With enough skill, we can precisely measure the seeds, weigh them, and study them. No amount of skill, though, can bring the seeds to life. Only the Holy Spirit can do that.

This is true of any word from God that lands in our hearts—whether it's a word voiced through the Scriptures or through nature or through the circumstances of our lives. Each and every word that comes to us will lie dormant in the soil unless the Spirit gives it life. And there it will wait...quiet and still...for the rain. [5]

The Longer the Wait, the Greater the Work

Just as an artist's body of work would bear certain stylistic similarities whether she worked with oil paints or watercolors, so the way God works in the natural world bears similarities to the way he works in the spiritual world.

The German poet Rilke was a student of both worlds. In a letter to a young poet, he explained that the natural process of becoming an artist was "to ripen like the tree which does not force its sap and stands confident in the storms...without fear."

To ripen, either as an artist or as a human being or as a Christian, takes time. And the greater the thing that is being grown, the more time is necessary for its ripening. Love, joy, peace, patience, and kindness are all fruit of the Spirit. And they all take time to reach fruition. The only fruit that doesn't take time to produce is artificial fruit, which has neither the taste nor the nutrition of real fruit, nor the seeds to reproduce itself.

Children are gifts God gives us (Psalm 127:3). The gestation period is nine months. Why so long? Because God is not only preparing a baby for the outside world; he is preparing the outside world for the baby. Month by month God is preparing a place in the parents' home and in their hearts. And that takes time. A lot of time. And a lot of thought…and conversations…and prayers. Even tears. They are all necessary to give the baby a nurturing environment in which to ripen as a human being.

To ripen from childhood to adulthood in the faith also takes time.

And faith.

The faith is not in the one who sows or in the one who waters or even in the one who waits. The faith is in the Word of God that has been planted in our heart (James 1:21) and in God, who causes the growth (1 Corinthians 3:6-7), knowing that he who has begun a good work in us will oversee the growth and bring it to fruition (Philippians 1:6). [6]

Waiting in the Tomb?

The steps of the dance lead us to the cross.

At the cross we see how Jesus lost his life and something of how we are to lose ours. It was his responsibility to die. It was the Father's responsibility to resurrect him. To us has been given a similar responsibility. Not to bring life out of death. But to die. Our responsibility is to surrender. The result of our surrender is not our responsibility. Understanding the truth of that has been liberating. It has also been sobering, because dying is the ultimate surrender of control, not only in the physical sense but also in the daily dying to self that we are all called to do.

What if in our daily lives we started living like Jesus did—dying to ourselves, giving of ourselves, surrendering ourselves?

But what happens if we do and God doesn't come through for us? What if he overlooks our surrender? What if he doesn't resurrect those moments of faith when we place the results in his hands to do with what he pleases, when he pleases? What then?

Then we wait in the tomb another day.

And another if necessary.

For as many days as God appoints.

Our days are in his hands, not ours. He appoints them all—the day of our birth, the day of our death, and the day of our resurrection. And not only the day of our physical resurrection but also all the other resurrections after the daily deaths to which we surrender ourselves—those days are in his hands as well.

Not only are the days of our lives in God's hands but also the shaping of our lives. All these incremental surrenderings of self are parts of the process God uses in shaping us into the image of his Son. Jesus was a man of sorrows, we are told. That was part of his beauty. Our sorrows acquaint us with his sorrows. Apart from suffering, there is a part of Jesus we cannot know. If there is a part of him we cannot know, there is a part of him we cannot love. And if there is a part of him we cannot love, there is a part of us that can never be beautiful.

At least here on earth. [7]

Darkness on the Mountain

Darkness is a somber chapter in mountain-climbing literature. Darkness must be anticipated and prepared for, but most of all it must be endured. A similar type of darkness—this time spiritual—is a theme in the psalms. Nowhere is that theme more fully developed than in Psalm 88.

The superscription of the psalm reads, "For the choir director: A psalm of the descendants of Korah. A song to be sung to the tune 'The Suffering of Affliction.' A psalm of Heman the Ezrahite."

Several things strike me about this superscription. It is a deeply personal psalm, forged on the anvil of affliction. Another thing that strikes me is the note to the choir director indicating the tune to which the lyrics should be sung. It seems remarkable to me that a tune such as "The Suffering of Affliction" would exist.

Even more striking than the prelude is the pathos of the psalm. Heman the Ezrahite prays and prays and prays, but his prayers go unanswered. He is deserted and despondent—no answer comes. No strong arm of the Almighty is bared to help him. No ray of light comes from heaven to illuminate his circumstances. There is not one word of praise in the psalm. Not one word of thanksgiving. Not one word of hope. And at the end of the psalm, it is not God's unfailing love that remains—it is darkness.

The Hebrew word translated "darkness" is *mahshak*, derived from the word *chôshek*. It appears only in poetic passages. In verse 6, it refers to the dark place that is the grave. Darkness here is synonymous with death. It is a place where all faith, all hopes, all dreams have been buried.

It is a place we will all come to at some point in our lives.

Even though Heman feels that God has turned his back on him, he doesn't turn his back on God. He cries out, but he cries out to God. He raises questions, but he raises them to God.

I don't know when your dark night on the mountain will come or how long it will last when it does. I don't have a formula to get you through it, or five keys to faithfulness in the midst of complete abandonment, or time-tested techniques to help you survive the night.

The darkness strips us of our keys, our formulas, our techniques. It steals them and tosses them down the side of the mountain. And though we feel we can't make the climb without them, the truth is that they were some of the very things that weighed us down and held us back. [8]

With Us Through the Night

Maybe the way God speaks to us is not terribly far off from the way we speak to our children.

All of us have experienced moments of hearing God's voice. We may not have understood it, but we sensed him speaking, sensed he was calling our name. Some of those moments may have been in dreams. He may tell us how proud he is to be our Father. A kid needs to hear that. A lot. He tells us that often throughout the day, but sometimes bedtime is the best time to hear it, when all the toys are put up and the books are back on the shelves and the spirit is still.

In some of those dreams, God whispers words of counsel just as any wise father would when his children are confused. In others, he shakes us the same way any good father would when his children are in danger. Still other times, God stops by our room in the middle of the night, tucks the covers up around our chin, kisses us on the forehead, and in our ear whispers something that to a sleepy ear sounds a lot like "I love you."

Those are the best dreams, the ones that make us want to never wake up.

And one day we won't. One day, all of this life will seem to have been the dream.

One day we will feel a hand brushing across our cheek and

a voice calling our name, and our eyes will open as if from a long sleep, and on our bedside we will see him whom we have longed all of our lives to see. And then we will realize, maybe for the first time, that he was not only there when we woke up in the morning, but he was with us all through the night. [9]

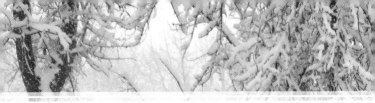

CHAPTER THREE

A Season's Storm

The storm that ripped past Elijah on the mountain eventually gave way to God's quiet whisper. Could the same happen for us?

Beyond the Clouds

When least expected, the still-gray sky gives way to billowing clouds. Storms of winter—from which nature bows and hides—arise angry and cold. Whether a blizzard, a hailstorm, or a mixture of rain and sleet, the storm appears to be too much to bear.

When facing the frigid winter storms of life, it is nigh impossible to picture anything beyond the difficulty of the moment, the severity of the trial. At times like these we wonder whether the sun was just a passing dream. Was there ever a time that it brought warmth to our hearts and life to our souls?

Trees that have endured the fiercest storms atop high mountains are carved into the sweetest-sounding violins. Nothing matches their quality and tone. A heart that has borne the severest tempests of life manifests an otherworldly grace, an unmatched tone, a lasting resonance.

Storms will rise, sent by the giver of all good things, even those things that we might not understand at the moment. The tears of the sky will be reflected on our faces and in the depth of our hearts.

Yet the sun does exist, and is shining with the same blaze it has always shone with. The clouds will part, the billows will pass, and the warmth will dry the tears from your face and bring life to the soil of your soul.

The Unfailing Rope

I don't know where you are on the mountain or what put you there. I don't know how wearied you are by the climb or how weathered you are by the elements. I don't know how alone or abandoned you feel. I don't know how disoriented you are or how despondent. But wherever you are and however you feel, I want you to curl up in your tent, close your eyes…and remember.

Remember your own history with God. Think back on the times when God expressed his love for you. Remember those times? Remember the words he spoke? Remember the way he answered your prayers? Remember the gifts he gave you? The many kindnesses he showed you? The forgiveness? The protection? Remember the love you felt for him, the joy, the tears? Remember how he touched you, embraced you, and led you?

He hasn't changed. Neither has his love for you. It may not seem to be there, just as a rope around your waist doesn't seem to be there when it's slack. But it is there. Paul told us that nothing—*nothing!*—would ever be able to separate us from the love of God that is revealed in Christ Jesus (Romans 8:35-39).

God's love for us, not ours for him, is the rope around our waist.

It's a rope that doesn't fray regardless of how much it is stretched.

It doesn't freeze regardless of how cold it gets.

It doesn't fail regardless of how far we fall…or how often. [1]

Near to the Broken

When the Messiah appeared, he came to the bruised reeds and dimly burning wicks of this world. To the sick, not the healthy. To those who had been devastated by life-shattering losses. To a demon-possessed man who had lost his mind. To a woman at a well who had lost her reputation. To a leper who had lost his health. To a mother who had lost her son.

Here is the story of that mother.

> Soon afterwards He went to a city called Nain; and His disciples were going along with Him, accompanied by a large crowd. Now as He approached the gate of the city, a dead man was being carried out, the only son of his mother, and she was a widow; and a sizeable crowd from the city was with her. When the Lord saw her, He felt compassion for her, and said to her, "Do not weep." And He came up and touched the coffin; and the bearers came to a halt. And He said, "Young man, I say to you, arise!" The dead man sat up and began to speak. And Jesus gave him back to his mother. Fear gripped them all, and they began

glorifying God, saying, "A great prophet has arisen among us!" and, "God has visited His people!" (Luke 7:11-16).

The miracle is an incredible display of the Savior's power. But there is something even more incredible about this auspicious meeting at the town gate.

This mother had not asked for a miracle. She had not thrown herself at the Savior's feet and begged for the life of her son. She hadn't demonstrated great faith. In fact, she hadn't demonstrated any faith at all. As far as we know, she didn't even know who Jesus was. Even so, he was drawn to her. Her brokenness is what drew him.

And what draws him still. [2]

Communion of Tears

Perhaps there are no greater windows of the soul than our tears. The tears we cry are drawn from the well of who we are, a well that lies beneath the sedimentary strata of words, beneath even the Precambrian layer of consciousness itself. They may seep to the surface like the smallest of subterranean springs or shoot to the surface like a geyser. They surface for odd reasons, or for no reason at all, or for reasons so pure and right and good that no force on earth could hold them back.

I think of the tears I have cried over the years, and by pooling them into one place, I can see rippling in it a reflection of myself.

Each tearful moment is a window. In each of those windows is something that not only sanctifies the moment but also transcends it. In each tear is distilled something of eternity, something of love and compassion and tenderness, all things that originate in heaven and come to earth as sacraments to my soul if only I am willing to take and eat.

The closest communion with God comes, I believe, through the sacrament of tears. Just as grapes are crushed to make wine and grain to make bread, so the crushing experiences of life produce the elements of this sacrament.

So much is distilled in our tears, not the least of which is wisdom in living life. From my own tears I have learned that if you follow your tears, you will find your heart. If you find your heart, you will find what is dear to God. And if you find what is dear to God, you will find the answer to how you should live your life. [3]

Beautiful Upheavals

Upheavals come suddenly, unexpectedly, and often catastrophically. Whenever they come, however they come, they forever alter the settled terrain of our lives. Embedded within us are physical, spiritual, and psychological layers that make up our interior landscape. When upheavals come, they alter every layer with varying degrees of destruction that sometimes take a lifetime to unearth.

Imagine for a minute that you are the landscape. The upheaval thrusts itself mercilessly through the very center of who you are. The abrading of granite. The crumbling of limestone. The crashing of boulders as they tumble down around you, shattering to pieces. You feel all of that, every grinding moment of it.

Your body, mind, emotions…all these layers are displaced. They are folded or pushed upward or thrust over each other. The social layers of your life are also shaken. And the spiritual layers that once seemed bedrock certainties, they're shaken too.

Where is God in all of this? Didn't he see the upheaval coming? Couldn't he have prevented it? Or at least warned us of it?

Much the way pressure within the earth thrusts rock formations through its crust to create mountains, the seismic pressure of these unanswered questions creates sudden and sometimes terrifying upheavals in our faith.

To this bare and broken rock, God comes.

There the weathering grace of God begins its work, wearing granite into soil, planting windblown seeds into barren slopes, bringing life out of lifelessness, beauty out of ugliness.

Season after season, the work continues.

In time, God turns the most terrifying of eruptions into the most majestic of mountains, the most tragic of earthquakes into the most idyllic of landscapes.

That is the unrelenting work of heaven—to make everything beautiful in its time. [4]

Embracing His Fellowship

I want to be like Christ. But honestly, I want to be like the Christ who turned the water into wine, not the Christ who thirsted on a cross. I want to be the clothed Christ, not the One whose garment was stripped off and gambled away. I want to be the Christ who fed the five thousand, not the One who hungered for forty days in the wilderness. I want to be the free Christ, walking through wheat fields with his disciples, not the imprisoned Christ, who was deserted by them.

I want to be the good Samaritan, not the man who fell among thieves.

But if the man had not fallen among thieves and been beaten, stripped, and left for dead, the good in the Samaritan never would have emerged.

If we want to be like Christ, we have to embrace both sides of his life. What else could the Bible mean when it talks about "the fellowship of his sufferings"? How could we enter that fellowship apart from suffering? How could we truly know the man of sorrows who was acquainted with grief if we had not ourselves known grief and sorrow?

That is how Christ grows in us. It is also the way many people come to Christ. For some people, it is the only way.

And perhaps that explains, at least partially, why bad things sometimes happen to good people.

For the sake of those around them. That they might come to Christ. That Christ might come to them, to live in them.

So that once again a Savior can be born into the world. [5]

The Sorrows of a Tool

The heart that loves is a heart that has been made vulnerable by its loving. The more people we love, the more we will suffer. And the deeper our love, the deeper our suffering.

At some time, in some way, I have suffered with each of my children. Suffered when one had been rejected by a classmate, when another had been rejected by a college. Suffered when one had a broken arm, when another had a broken heart. Suffered when they cried each time we moved, leaving old friends behind, and suffered as they struggled making new ones.

I want their pain to cease. But I know that their sorrows and their joys will shape them into growing levels of understanding.

I try to hold on to them, to each of our four children, who are now grown and out of the house. But I know I must let them go. In many ways I have. Still, it's not easy.

They must live their lives, going wherever the hand of God leads them. They must experience their own joys, their own sorrows. Their own loves, their own losses. Still, I want to protect them from the pain that awaits them. Partly for their sakes. Partly also for mine, to protect me from the pain that their pain will inevitably bring me.

Suffering is part of the process God uses in shaping us. I have come to the understanding that if I spare my children from the suffering, I will also be sparing them from the shaping. In doing so, I will be sparing them from the fellowship of Christ's suffering, from the deeper understanding that awaits them there, the deeper love that awaits them there, the deeper gratitude. And, as incongruous as it seems, the deeper joy.

This I have come to know is true. My children are not the work of my hands. My hands are not the hands that hold them, not the hands that mold them, not the hands that work all things together in their lives for good. They are the work of *God's* hands. I am merely a tool in those hands, a tool he has used in some way, for a short time, to shape them.

Though merely a tool, I am a tool that loves them. And though the tool may be used only in some way and only for a short time, it will love them in all ways and for all time. Even after the tool wears out and has been put away, the love it once had for them will live on in them.

There has been joy in having my children at home, and sorrow in letting them go. Those feelings, I have come to understand, are also tools, tools that God has used in some way, for a short time, in shaping me. [6]

Mystery, Ambiguity, Uncertainty... Comfort

Who we are, who we truly are, is a secret known only to God. One day we will be given the stone that bears our new name (Revelation 2:17). But today, that name is a mystery, even to us. Mystery is an unsettling concept. I think we feel if we can somehow connect all the dots in life in some kind of cause-and-effect manner, life can be managed and made safe for us and for those we love.

But the universe cannot be managed or made safe. Not by us anyway. When we lose a sense of mystery, we lose a sense of our place in the universe. And leaving that place, we leave behind a humility that is attendant to that place.

Mystery, ambiguity, uncertainty. These are places where we reach an end of ourselves, places where we have to stop, stop and take off our shoes. If we don't, the mystery, the ambiguity, the uncertainty will one day prove too much for us. If we must have all our questions answered before we can go forward in our relationship with God, there will come a day when we won't go forward.

Who knows what day that one question will go unanswered?

All we know is that one day it will. It did for Jesus. And it will for us.

In the meantime, we are surrounded by mystery. Who we are is a mystery. What role we play in the unfolding drama of redemption is also a mystery. How long we will play that role is a mystery too. Some mysteries remain God's secrets. Others Jesus shares with us.

Our lives are part of an overarching drama—part sunshine, part rain—that spans the heavens from paradise to paradise. What role we play in that drama is a secret Jesus shares with us, if at all, at his own discretion. The most personal secrets of our story are seldom shared with anyone else.

For now we see in a glass darkly, but then face-to-face, and now we know in part, but then we shall know fully just as we have been fully known (1 Corinthians 13:12).

So until then, what?

We feel our way in the dark.

Until we find each other.

We huddle together in the storm.

Wet and shivering, but together.

And maybe in the end it will be our huddling in the storm that gives us more comfort than our understanding of the storm. [7]

Dancing Through Dissonance

We have been invited to dance, not to choreograph.

Still, the more dissonant the dance, the harder it is to believe that there is any choreographer behind the steps, let alone a divine one. It seems the steps are a mistake and that the best thing to do is to get through that part as quickly as we can. Perhaps longer strides or faster footwork are what we need.

That's seldom the case.

Then what do we need? When the room starts to spin and we feel as if we are falling away, what do we do? How do we get through those parts? We get through them the same way Jesus got through them. How dizzy he must have felt the night of his betrayal, when he was caught in the spin of those circumstances. What did he do to get through it? He drew closer, and he held on tighter. He got alone with his Father, threw himself at his feet, begging to sit out the steps that lay ahead, but finally surrendering to the dissonant rhythms the Father was leading him through, however difficult they were to follow.

Drawing closer, holding on tighter.

That is what Gethsemane was all about.

That is what the upper room was about. Jesus drawing the disciples closer and embracing them tighter than ever before. Even so, they all fell away (Mark 14:27,50). Even the one most determined not to (verses 29-31). After his resurrection, Jesus returned to them as he had promised (verse 28). At one time or another he returned to all of them (1 Corinthians 15:5). He returned to the two despondent disciples on the road to Emmaus (Luke 24). To his brother James (1 Corinthians 15:7). To Peter and others (John 21:1-17).

Why did he return? He returned to restore some of the old rhythms that had broken down in the transition, but also to introduce them to some of the new rhythms he would be leading them in (see Acts 1:1-8).

I still love you, he seems to be saying to Peter when he returned to him. I still love you, even though you fell away, even though you stumbled, even though you stepped on my toes. I still love you, and I still want to dance with you. [8]

Struggle of Seasons

I called out desperately to hear God during my long night in the woods. I called for direction, for understanding, for help. I asked for a way out, and if not a way out, at least a footprint letting me know he was somewhere in the woods with me, a broken twig, something, anything. I had certainly been lonely enough in my depression, but had I been attentive enough?

It was a day that lent itself to being attentive when I finally did hear something, or thought I did. There was six inches of snow. I walked in the backyard, stood, looked, listened.

The snow muffled everything, making everything seem distant, seeming as if the world had stepped back to give you room, to give you a space of your own where thought of your own could stretch and move around.

I saw plants pushing their way through the snow, struggling to be green, or so it seemed as I watched them. Two seasons were competing for the same ground. Spring struggling to be born. Winter struggling not to die. And it seemed to me some sort of parable.

Then the husk of the parable opened up, revealing a kernel of truth. Something inside me was struggling to be born. Something else was struggling not to die. And they were both inside me at the same time, winter and spring, contesting each other. The ending of one was necessary for the beginning of the other. A new beginning. I sensed it, sensed a seasonal shift within me. A stirring of the soil. A feeling that some germinating seed was unfurling itself.

Depression is a burying of the soul in the ground, where it waits in the cold, lonely darkness, silent, solitary, waiting for the coming of spring, the warmth of the sun, and the companionship of all living things. "Unless a grain of wheat falls into the earth and dies, it remains alone." Depression, I learned, is not only the dark soil into which the grain falls but also the soil out of which grows the fruit.

But what fruit had grown out of that soil?

The bittersweet knowledge of how little control I had over life, even my very own life, how little control any of us have over the storms that come into our lives or into the lives of those we love. Sometimes all you can do is to hold on for dear life until the storm passes.

Slowly, an empathy for others grew from all this, an understanding I didn't have before, a compassion. And the tears allowed me to touch the hem of Christ's sorrows. It was a very small hem and a very brief touch, but it gave me a greater understanding of the sadness he carried with him as he walked this earth. And with that understanding came a deeper love. [9]

Is God an Everest?

As god of this world, the enemy cannot control our hearts, but he can control the weather that wisps around us. Clouds are everywhere. So is the wind, the cold, and the snow. When our spiritual eyes are blinded by the sleet, when our feelings are frostbitten, when our thoughts are disoriented by the altitude, we are in no shape to make judgments, least of all judgments about God.

Those judgments distort the picture of who God is—with disastrous consequences. When the serpent came to Adam and Eve, he showed them a distorted picture of God. Based on that picture, they turned their backs on their Creator.

If you picture God as an Everest of indifference, the enemy has won the battle for your heart. That was the battle C.S. Lewis came close to losing when his wife died. "Not that I am (I think) in much danger of ceasing to believe in God," he wrote. "The real danger is of coming to believe such dreadful things about Him. The conclusion I dread is not, 'So there's no God after all,' but, 'So this is what God's really like. Deceive yourself no longer.'"

What we supposed was the North Face of God was merely the steepness of the slopes of a fallen world and the cold realities swirling around it. Although the climbing principles remain the same, the identity of the mountain does not. God is not and never was an Everest of indifference, although the sleet of suffering can sometimes create that illusion.

So how do we protect ourselves against such distortion?

By keeping a clear picture of God with us at all times.

And how do we do that?

The writer to the Hebrews tells us to look to Jesus, for he "radiates God's own glory and expresses the very character of God" (Hebrews 1:3). If you have seen me, Jesus told his disciples, you have seen the Father (John 14:9).

The Word became flesh so we could gaze into eyes brimming with the compassion that God has for us and for the losses we have experienced; so we could feel a heart throbbing with the love he has for us; so we could touch skin tingling with the excitement he has for the wholeness of our lives and the fullness of our futures.

Everywhere Jesus went, he left behind pictures that showed us who God is (John 1:18). And what is the composite of those pictures? A God who sees and who cares. A God who listens and who speaks. Who touches and transforms. A God who calms the wind, stills the waves, and extends his hand to the sinking. A God who heals the sick and raises the dead. Who frees the prisoners, feeds the hungry, blesses the children. A God who came at the greatest personal cost to destroy the works of the devil.

Hardly an Everest of indifference. [10]

The Broken Jar

The winds of treachery have been gusting around Jesus with increasing intensity. But there is a calm eye in the midst of this storm of mounting opposition. It is a home in Bethany, a shelter of intimate friends who come to honor him.

Yet a draft has made its way into this warm circle of friends, and betrayal is in the air. Still, only Christ feels the chill. Christ and one other—Mary.

She comes with perfume. Expensive perfume. As she anoints him, the aroma of extravagant love fills the room. So pure. So lovely. Flowing from the veined alabaster jar of her heart, a heart broken against the hard reality of her Savior's imminent death.

Her actions are strangely out of place, a breech not only of etiquette but of a woman's place in this culture. And yet…are not her actions the most appropriate? Is not the breech instead being committed by the men?

Did they not see the shadow of the cross lengthening to overtake their Lord? Did they not know his hour was fast upon him?

Time and again, Jesus warned them. Both in parable—of the tenants killing the landowner's son—and in plain language.

> We're going up to Jerusalem, where the Son of
> Man will be betrayed to the leading priests and
> teachers of religious law. They will sentence
> him to die and hand him over to the Romans.
> They will mock him, spit on him, flog him
> with a whip, and kill him (Mark 10:33-34).

How much clearer could he have spoken? What were these men thinking? Were the words so painful that they suppressed them? Or their minds so occupied with the work of the kingdom that they lost sight of their King?

For the disciples, the ministry was fast becoming a business to be budgeted rather than a Savior to be served.

What a stab in the heart this must have been to their honored guest. Bickering about the poor when one sits in their midst famished for a crust of human understanding. They are his most intimate confidants, yet none has a clue to the gnawing hunger inside him. Peter doesn't. James doesn't. John doesn't.

But Mary, she does. She sees the melting tallow of emotions in Christ's eyes. So beautiful the flame. So tender the wick. So mercenary the hand that seeks to extinguish it.

For this brief candle she weeps. And as she does, she anoints him with perfume to prepare for his burial.

Soon the body of Jesus would be broken. Blood would spill from the whip, from the thorns, from the nails...and finally, from the spear thrust in his side.

A perfume more precious than nard. So pure. So lovely. So truly extravagant.

The Savior had come to earth to break an alabaster jar for humanity. And Mary had come that night to break one for him.

It was a jar he never regretted breaking.

Nor did she. [11]

Broken Hallelujah

When we experience the silence of God in the midst of our suffering, our interpretation of that silence often adds to the tyranny. To be alone in our struggles, alone in our suffering, cuts us off from a major avenue of God's grace.

There is a hauntingly beautiful contemporary hymn by Leonard Cohen titled "Hallelujah." If you've seen the movie *Shrek*, you've heard it. The hymn talks about David's life, his confusion, and his sin with Bathsheba. And then the lyricist integrates his own life into the song, his own joys, his own sorrows, his own struggle to make sense of who God is. Each stanza ends with a chorus of hallelujahs.

The word "hallelujah" comes from two Hebrew words: *hallel*, which means "praise," and *jah*, which is an abbreviation for Yahweh, or Lord. It literally means "praise the Lord."

In Cohen's hymn, the praise comes from a baffled king, its incongruous rhythms rising out of the moral chaos and confusions of his life. Halfway through the song, it says that love is not a triumphant parade but rather a cold and broken hallelujah.

When hope and history don't rhyme—especially the hope and history of our own lives—it creates a chasm of opposing realities. The way to bridge that chasm is with our hallelujahs, however cold those hallelujahs feel…or however broken.

Dear Lord,

*Give me the grace to praise you in the heartbreaks,
no matter how cold and broken the hallelujah.* [12]

CHAPTER FOUR

A Season's Promise

Through the long nights and the
dreary days, there is always that hope,
the promise of spring.

A Mosaic of Redemption

Years after his historic Everest ascent, Tenzing Norgay would tell his son, "You can't see the entire world from the top of Everest, Jamling. The view from there only reminds you how big the world is and how much more there is to see and learn."

The curvature of the earth limits how much we can see, even from the summit of the world's tallest mountain on a clear day. Likewise, from the summit of biblical revelation, we can see the far reaches of the promises made to Abraham and to David, but with respect to the promises made to us, the curvature of time limits our seeing beyond the hand width of our own lives.

Here and there we are given glimpses of those promises the way some of the people in the Bible were given glimpses.

Dietrich Bonhoeffer, the German Lutheran pastor who was sent to a concentration camp and later executed for his participation in a plot to overthrow Adolf Hitler, reached a summit of understanding about life that few on the foothills of Christian experience ever come to. As he was being crushed under the jackbooted heel of the Third Reich, he reflected on his life, which seemed like so many inconsequential fragments lying in the dirt. He wrote this just months before his death.

It all depends on whether or not the fragment of our life reveals the plan and material of the whole. There are fragments which are only good to be thrown away, and others which are important for centuries to come because their fulfillment can only be a divine work. They are fragments of necessity. If our life, however remotely, reflects such a fragment…we shall not have to bewail our fragmentary life, but, on the contrary, rejoice in it.

From our brief time on earth, it is hard for us to know which parts of our lives are fragments to be thrown away and which parts are fragments of necessity, reflecting a divine work that may be centuries in the making.

When suffering shatters the carefully kept vase that is our lives, God stoops to pick up the pieces. But he doesn't put them back together as a restoration project patterned after our former selves. Instead, he sifts through the rubble and selects some of the shards as raw material for another project—a mosaic that tells the story of redemption.

Despite how the curvature of time has limited our view, from the summit of biblical revelation we can see the entire span of biblical history and the faithfulness of God in keeping his promises. That is the basis of our hope—not simply for us but also for our children. And our children's children. And all the generations after them, on into eternity. [1]

The Fragrance of His Voice

The Bible begins and ends in paradise. In between the Garden of Eden and the garden in the New Jerusalem lies a sprawling landscape.

In the life of Israel, the landscape stretches from Ur to Egypt, winds around Mount Sinai, through a wilderness, into a land flowing with milk and honey, out into exile, and eventually back to Palestine.

The life of Christ traces other terrain. There is a wilderness too, only a different one. And heavenly words are also revealed on a mountain, only not on tablets of stone but in words of a sermon, words that give those spoken on Mount Sinai even greater resonance. On another mountain, a higher mountain, his glory is revealed. There is a valley through which he passes, a garden in which he prays, and a hill on which he dies.

Our own lives, yours and mine, pass through a similar geography of the soul, with its pinnacles of faith and its valleys of doubt, its plateaus of complacency, its wildernesses of spiritual dryness.

Along the way, God speaks. In the peak experiences of our lives. In the valleys. On the plateaus. Even in the wilderness, where all traces of him seem to have vanished.

He has much to say, not only from the Scriptures but from the circumstances of our everyday lives. However prosaic the pages of our lives may seem at first reading, within the lines or in between the lines, God may be speaking.

Sometimes the voice of God thunders into our lives, but more often than not, it wisps by us like a gentle breeze with a fragrant reminder in it of faraway fields.

So relax and reflect…
not only on the biblical landscape
but on the landscape of your life. [2]

Homesick for Heaven

Every sorrow, every tear, every loss, every death reminds us that this is not our home. Every ache and pain whispers to us, "You were made from dust, and to dust you will return" (Genesis 3:19). We long for the promise of security, but we know it's a promise that nothing on this earth can fulfill.

Like the children of Israel, we long for a Promised Land, where we will be safe and secure. Certainly Moses, their leader, longed for it. In Psalm 90, the only psalm of Moses recorded in the Bible, he speaks from the perspective of a man looking back on his life, dizzy at how quickly it all sped by, the way a dream dissipates upon waking.

The patriarch prays for himself and for his children after him, praying that the song they sing at the end of their lives might be a joyful one, that the misery they have experienced will be balanced out by happy experiences, that the evil years will be replaced with a few good ones.

Not a bad thing to long for. But what he really longs for, I think, is more than that. What I think he longs for is home.

Where is home for Moses? Is it the palatial estate in Egypt? Is it the peaceful meadows of his father-in-law's fields? Is it the Promised Land of Canaan?

I don't think so. I think the home he longs for is found in verse 1:

"Lord, through all the generations you have been our home!"

Imagine it. To have God as our home! That is where we are secure and safe. That is where we are happy and at peace. In God's presence. That is the home Moses longs for, the one we all long for. And that is the home that the apostle John described in Revelation 21:3-4.

> I heard a loud shout from the throne, saying, "Look, God's home is now among his people! He will live with them, and they will be his people. God himself will be with them. He will wipe every tear from their eyes, and there will be no more death or sorrow or crying or pain. All these things are gone forever."

Maybe the summit of understanding we long for is not an answer to our questions about suffering. Maybe the summit is that place where the suffering ends—not just our suffering but all suffering. And where the silence ends too.

Who knows, maybe without the suffering and the silence, we might mistake this inn-along-the-way for home. And if we found our security and happiness here on earth, we might never look for it elsewhere. We might never find God. We might never have a home to miss, let alone to come home to. [3]

Sacrament from Heaven

The life we have been given can't be bought or bargained for. It is a gift. Every good and perfect gift comes from above, James tells us, coming down from the Father of lights in whom there is no variation or shifting shadow (James 1:17). If our day is indeed a gift from God, something of the Giver should be evident within that gift.

It is a great loss that we awake to so many gifts on a given day, not only without opening them but without knowing they are even there for us to open. When each of us awakes, it should be with a splash-of-cold-water-in-the-face awareness: *I have been given another day to live. Another day to give gifts and to receive them. To love and to be loved.*

Each new morning that God's mercies dawn on us with the gift of another day, we should greet that day with an attitude of expectant reverence, as one kneeling to receive the sacrament of some holy communion, for truly it is.

Sacraments are ordinary things through which something extraordinary is offered. An ordinary bush ablaze with God's glory. Tablets of earthly stone engraved by a heavenly hand. The divine Word becoming flesh and dwelling among us.

If God does still speak, perhaps some of those words are words for us. Something from heaven offered to us through earthly hands.

Coming to us like sacrament.

Letting us know that we are looked after and that we are loved. [4]

Standing in the Shadow

I have had moments when I seemed to be at the railing that separates heaven and earth, and there was offered a sacrament. The sacrament may have been some hauntingly beautiful music or the echo of an elk bugling in the mountains. It may have been a freshly-cut-peach sunset or a crayoned work of refrigerator art. It may have been a verse of Scripture or a line from Shakespeare.

Whatever your moments have been, you sensed that something sacred was being offered you. Receiving them, you knew somehow and with great certainty that this was not your home, that your home was the place where your deepest longings were leading you, somewhere beyond the fields we know, somewhere that is beautiful beyond telling.

Someday not only will we become beautiful, but the whole creation will become beautiful (Romans 8:18-22). Stunningly beautiful. For eye has not seen, nor ear heard, nor mind imagined all that God has prepared for those who love him (1 Corinthians 2:9). The beauty of the most breathtaking mountains here is but a shadow of what awaits us there.

John Muir believed that God did his best work in the mountains. He wrote that "the rocks where the exposure to storms is the greatest, and where only ruin seems to be the object, are all the more lavished upon with beauty."

Those who have endured this weathering grace of God are not hard and craggy but are those whose edges have been smoothed and whose faces have been softened. In the vast range of people I have known over my life, these are not only the most beautiful but also the most companionable in times of storm. [5]

Likeness of the King

Windows of the soul are where God finds us, or where we find him, depending on whose point of view we're looking from. He comes to us where we are, speaks to us in our own language, calls us by our name.

In the past, God's word has come through tablets of stone and handwriting on a wall and through the pages of Scripture. It has come through a flood and a rainbow, a burning bush and a whirling wind. His word has thundered from Sinai and whimpered from a manger. His word was spoken through the law of Moses and afterward, more eloquently, through the life of Christ.

Some of those words are spoken at such unexpected places that if we're not expecting them, we'll miss them.

Those words are the daily bread of our soul.

What we hear at the windows of the soul may daze us or delight us. It may cause us to fall to our knees in fear or jump to our feet in joy. Sometimes what we hear at those windows is merely something to help us understand people more deeply or experience life more fully. Other times, what we hear are simple words of great authority that God has spoken.

It seems only appropriate to kneel in the presence of such words.

It seems too that these words, which are often beyond the human tongue to tell, should produce in us a momentary likeness of the King. [6]

The Promised King

For the census, the royal family has to travel eighty-five miles. Joseph walks, while Mary, nine months pregnant, rides sidesaddle on a donkey, feeling every jolt, every rut, every rock in the road.

By the time they arrive, the small hamlet of Bethlehem is swollen from an influx of travelers. The inn is packed, people feeling lucky if they were able to negotiate even a small space on the floor. Now it is late, everyone is asleep, and there is no room.

But fortunately, the innkeeper is not all shekels and mites. True, his stable is crowded with his guests' animals, but if they could squeeze out a little privacy there, they were welcome to it.

The birth would not be easy, either for the mother or the child. For every royal privilege for this Son ended at conception. Mary has to push with all her strength, almost as if God were refusing to come into the world without her help.

Joseph places a garment beneath her, and with a final push and a long sigh, her labor is over.

The Messiah has arrived.

The baby chokes and coughs. Then he cries. Mary bares her breast and reaches for the shivering baby. She lays him on her chest, and his helpless cries subside. His tiny head bobs around on the unfamiliar terrain. This will be the first thing the Infant-King learns. Mary can feel his racing heartbeat as he gropes to nurse.

Deity nursing from a young maiden's breast. Could anything be more puzzling—or more profound?

The baby finishes and sighs, the divine Word reduced to a few unintelligible sounds. Then, for the first time, his eyes fix on his mother's. Deity straining to focus. The light of the world, squinting.

Tears pool in her eyes. She touches his tiny hand. And hands that once sculpted mountain ranges cling to her finger.

And so, with barely a ripple of notice, God stepped into the warm lake of humanity. Without protocol and without pretension.

Where you would have expected angels, there were only flies. Where you would have expected heads of state, there were only donkeys, a few haltered cows, a nervous ball of sheep, a tethered camel, and a furtive scurry of curious barn mice.

Yes, there were angels announcing the Savior's arrival—but only to a band of blue-collar shepherds. And yes, a magnificent star shone in the sky to mark his birthplace—but only three foreigners bothered to look up and follow it.

Thus, in the little town of Bethlehem…that one silent night…the royal birth of God's Son tiptoed quietly by…as the world slept. [7]

Careless in His Care

Look at the birds, free and unfettered, not tied down to a job description, careless in the care of God. And you count far more to him than birds" (Matthew 6:26).

Careless in the care of God. And why shouldn't they be?

For their food, he provides insects in the air, seeds on the ground.

For their search for food, he provides eyes that are keen, wings that are swift.

For their drinking, he provides pools of rainwater.

For their bathing, he provides puddles.

For their survival, he provides migratory instincts to take them to warmer climates.

For their flight, he provides bones that are porous and lightweight.

For their warmth, he provides feathers.

For their dryness, he provides a water-resistant coating.

For their rest, he provides warm updrafts so they can glide through the air.

For their journey, he provides the company of other travelers.

For their return, he provides the companionship of a mate.

For their safety, he provides a perch in branches far from the reach of predators.

For their nest, he provides twigs.

And for every newborn beak, he provides enough worms so they can grow up to leave the nest and continue the cycle of life.

It's no wonder they're so free from the cares of this world.

The wonder is, if we count more to him than birds, why aren't we? [8]

A Promise of Beauty

He makes everything beautiful in its time." The words are Solomon's (Ecclesiastes 3:11). The "he" is God. The Hebrew word for "beautiful" is *yapheh*. It is the same word used in Genesis 12 to describe Sarah.

> Now there was a famine in the land; so Abram went down to Egypt to sojourn there, for the famine was severe in the land. It came about when he came near to Egypt, that he said to Sarai his wife, "See now, I know that you are a beautiful woman; and when the Egyptians see you, they will say, 'This is his wife'; and they will kill me, but they will let you live. Please say that you are my sister so that it may go well with me because of you, and that I may live on account of you." It came about when Abram came into Egypt, the Egyptians saw that the woman was very beautiful. Pharaoh's officials saw her and praised her to Pharaoh; and the woman was taken into Pharaoh's house. Therefore he treated Abram well for her sake; and gave him sheep and oxen and donkeys

and male and female servants and female donkeys and camels (verses 10-16).

Sarah was not just beautiful, she was *stunningly* beautiful.
Everywhere she went, heads turned.

God's purpose is to make us beautiful. How beautiful?
Stunningly beautiful. As beautiful as his Son in all his glory
(Romans 8:18-19,29-30).

There is much in this world to distract us from the splen-
dor of Christ's beauty. There is much in the church to distract
us. And much within ourselves. There is so much ugliness in
the world, and that is what sometimes distracts us. There is
ugliness in the church too. And within ourselves.

But there is no ugliness in Jesus. He is altogether beautiful. Someday the beauty that is his will be ours. For it has not
yet appeared what we shall be like, but when Jesus appears, we
shall see him as he is. And seeing him, we shall become like
him (1 John 3:2). [9]

A Stanza of Hope

As we walk among the ruins of our lives, can we hope that they will ever be rebuilt? When the enemy has trampled all that we hold sacred, when we are left to wander dazed among the rubble, when all our dreams have gone up in smoke, how can hope survive? When a spouse destroys the sanctuary of a twenty-year marriage, leaving the family in ruins, how can hope survive such an assault? When a family business goes bankrupt, reducing years of hard work to ashes, and the assets are carried into captivity by creditors, how can hope survive such a loss?

Regardless how sorrowful the song, there is always a stanza, if remembered, that can restore hope.

When World War II ended, this inscription was discovered on the wall of a cellar in Cologne, Germany, where Jews had hidden from the Nazis.

> I believe in the sun even when it is not shining.
> I believe in love even when feeling it not.
> I believe in God even when he is silent.

No matter how dark the night, how dense the clouds, or how total the eclipse, the sun is still at the center of our solar system, shining. So is God. Even though we can't see evidence of him through a miraculous sign or hear guidance from him through a prophetic voice, he is still there, in the center of all things. And he is still shining!

Here is our hope: that a day is coming when there will be no night, a day when all things will be made new. It will come because God is faithful in keeping his promises, both to his creation and to his covenant people. And here is something of what that day will look like:

> Then I saw a new heaven and a new earth, for the old heaven and the old earth had disappeared. And the sea was also gone. And I saw the holy city, the new Jerusalem, coming down from God out of heaven like a bride beautifully dressed for her husband...
>
> And the one sitting on the throne said, "Look, I am making everything new!"...
>
> No longer will there be a curse upon anything. For the throne of God and of the Lamb will be there, and his servants will worship him. And they will see his face, and his name will be written on their foreheads. And there will be no night there—no need for lamps or sun— for the Lord God will shine on them (Revelation 21:1-2,5; 22:3-5). [10]

Unbargained Beauty

God is using the circumstances of our lives as tools. He goes about his work the same way Michelangelo went about his when sculpting the Pietà. Within the rough-hewn stone of the self is trapped the image of Christ. To release the image, he chips away everything that isn't Jesus.

Just as the essence of sculpture is the loss of the stone, the essence of being conformed to the image of Christ is the loss of the self. For it is in losing the self, as Jesus said, that we find our best self, our most beautiful self, our truest self, our most eternal self. The self that is most like him.

We are God's workmanship, Paul says (Ephesians 2:10). That is the serious work of heaven. Making us like Christ. And God, as an impassioned artist, won't rest until that work is everything he envisioned it to be (Philippians 1:6).

We are the work of his hands, you and I. We are masterpieces in the making. And not just any masterpiece. His masterpiece.

The hands that work on us are God's hands. And just as Jesus worked beside his Father in the creation of the world, so he lends his hands in the crafting of our character. Those hands are something near, touching the contours of our soul. Other times they are far, searching for a different tool. At all times, though, they are purposeful. Their purpose is to make us beautiful.

The beauty of Christ is what we are destined for.

It is also more than we ever bargained for. [11]

A Promise of Peace

Between *Paradise Lost* and *Paradise Regained* is life as we now know it. That life is filled with all sorts of wonderful and terrible things, many of which are mirrored in the movies, some of which are mirrored in *Bambi*.

There are a lot of wonderful moments in *Bambi*, but there are terrible moments too. Like the moment when Bambi's mother is shot. After all these years I still remember that moment. I even remember my reaction to it.

It was the first time it had happened to me in a movie. It was the first time it had happened to me anywhere. I'm not sure if I cried. If I did, I didn't cry a lot or loudly. What I did do was this. I mourned. Truly mourned. Not just for Bambi's mother but for Bambi. Maybe even more for him.

The death of Bambi's mother took me by surprise. A part of me was sad. Another part of me was shaken. After all, it was a mother that was killed. Not a criminal. Not simply an animal. A mother. What kind of world is it where mothers are killed? What kind of world is it where innocent life is indiscriminately taken? Where children are left to fend for themselves?

The real world.

The world we live in isn't a fairy tale. Somehow I knew that, even as a child. The world we live in isn't Cinderella's world. Or

Snow White's world. Or Sleeping Beauty's. The real world is Bambi's world. What the movie had to say about life was true. Scary but true. And as strange as it sounds, knowing that was comforting. I think the movie validated the emerging feelings I had about the world I was living in. That, I think, was the source of my comfort, that I wasn't the only one who felt this way, that my truth lined up with somebody else's truth.

The film tells the truth, not only about life but about the season of life.

The films that speak to us in our childhood have enormous resonance in our adulthood. And whenever I think of *Bambi*, it evokes the tenderest and gentlest of feelings. Feelings I think we all will have, all the time, when at last the wolf will lie down with the lamb (Isaiah 11:6-9). When at last we will no longer hurt or destroy. When at last we will live with the deer and be as gentle as they are, existing together in peace, playing together as friends.

Then at last the whole forest will be happy.

And God will be happy too. [12]

Finding Fullness

We're starved for a life that not only senses the sacred in the world around us but savors it. We're famished for experiences that are real, relationships that are deep, work that is meaningful.

I think what we're longing for is not "the good life" as it has been advertised to us in the American dream, but life in its fullness, its richness, its abundance. Living more reflectively helps us enter into that fullness.

The reflective life is a life that is attentive, receptive, and responsive to what God is doing in us and around us. It's a life that asks God to reach into our hearts, allowing him to touch us there, regardless of the pleasure it excites or the pain it inflicts. It's a life that reaches back, straining to touch the hem of Christ's garment, allowing him to turn and call us out of the crowd, regardless of how humiliating it is to stand before him or how uncertain we are as to what he will say. Uncertain whether he will say, "O you of little faith," or "Your faith has made you well." Uncertain whether he will say, "Follow me," or "Where I am going you cannot follow."

Regardless of the uncertainty, we can be certain of this: The words he speaks are words of life. That is why we must reach for them, receive them, and respond to them. Whatever they may say, however they may sound, whatever implications they may have for our lives, the words that proceed from his mouth offer life to our souls.

Those words are how our relationship with God grows. Living reflectively is how we receive them. [13]

A Home over the Rainbow

The *Wizard of Oz* won two Academy Awards—one for best musical score, and one for best song, "Somewhere over the Rainbow," which was almost cut from the movie. A special award was given to Judy Garland for an outstanding performance by a teenager.

Something inside us longs for a faraway place where troubles melt like lemon drops and the dreams that we dare to dream really do come true.

When the sweet, sixteen-year-old Judy Garland sang this song, she sang it for all of us. It's my favorite moment in the film and the moment that set me dreaming for the place she sang about.

Someplace where there isn't any trouble. Do you suppose there could be such a place?

Jesus said there was. It's a real place, a real, true-life place (John 14:2), where there will no longer be any death or mourning or crying or pain (Revelation 21:4). The place is heaven. I believe we have an innate longing for it that is as deeply embedded in us as our genetic code.

The tornado plopped Dorothy's house down in the Land of Oz. When Dorothy opened the door, the drab monotone of the Kansas countryside was behind her. Before her stretched a world sparkling with color, the world of the Emerald City and the Yellow Brick Road and the Enchanted Forest. When you think about it, Oz seems less like a fairy tale and more like the land described in the final chapters of Revelation.

Little by little, my longing for heaven was stirred. First by that song in the movie and then by a series of books called The Chronicles of Narnia by C.S. Lewis. By the time we finished reading them, we all wanted to go to Narnia.

Heaven is our home. That is what we have been homesick for all of our lives. And if we must become children in order to get there, as Jesus insisted, then maybe the best preparation for that is not to be found in colleges and seminaries but in places like Narnia and Oz. Maybe the longings to go there don't come from textbooks but from songs. And maybe if the longings are strong enough, anything might take us there for a glimpse—a wardrobe, a tornado, even a moment at the movies.[14]

Chapter Five

A Season's Joy

Even in winter,
there still remains a little of the
magic that is life, and love, and joy—
moments of fun and wonder.

Delight of the Dance

Dancing is more than getting the steps right. It's about feeling the music and moving to the music. It's about losing ourselves in the embrace of someone we love. Above all, it's about joy.

There is satisfaction in getting the steps right. There is a thrill in the grand, sweeping movements of the dance. There is something gratifying about the acknowledgment of others. And yet…

The joy of the dance is not in the precision of our steps.

It's not in the exhilaration of being swept away.

It's not in the affirmation of the audience.

The joy of the dance is in the delight in our partners' eyes.

The dance of intimacy is more than just steps. It's about being in the Lord's arms as we follow his steps, close enough to his heart to feel the music. It's not about just being swept away, however good that feels. It's about being swept away by him. It's not about what others think of us; it's about what he thinks. And what he thinks is captured in his eyes.

When Jesus looks at us, regardless of how we feel about ourselves, he feels delight.

And that delight is in his eyes before we ever take our first step, just as the delight that God the Father had for his Son was in his eyes before Jesus took his first step. On the day of

Christ's baptism, a proud Father spoke out: "This is my Son, chosen and marked by my love, delight of my life" (Matthew 3:17). The Father delighted in Jesus before he died on the cross. He delighted in Jesus before he made his first disciple, before he preached his first sermon, before he performed his first miracle. Why? Because Jesus was his Son.

If you've ever had a child, you know.

The delight is there long before the first step. [1]

North to Gladness

Look back on your life and put frames around the things that brought you joy. Do you see the pictures? Look at them. Look closer. Deeper. Are they windows? If so, what is it you see in them? What is it you hear? A voice? What is that voice saying? And can you hear it above all the other voices that have called to you over the years?

Frederick Buechner asked similar questions in a graduation address.

> The voice we should listen to most as we choose a vocation is the voice that we might think we should listen to least, and that is the voice of our own gladness. What can we do that makes us the gladdest, what can we do that leaves us with the strongest sense of sailing true north and of peace, which is much of what gladness is?...I believe that if it is a thing that makes us truly glad, then it is a good thing and it is our thing and it is the calling voice that we were made to answer with our lives.

Seminary is a place where, of all places, I think, we should hear voices like that. I, for one, was too busy with schoolwork and supporting a family and ministry and trying to catch up on sleep to do much of that then. But now, as I look back, my greatest joy in seminary, what made me the gladdest, what left me with the strongest sense of sailing true north, was writing my master's thesis.

I was a writer, not a pastor. And if I had listened to my life, listened to the things that brought me joy, I would have known that. And I would have known it a long time ago, if only I had been looking.

We skip down the hallways of our youth, you and I, stopping now and then to catch our breath. And every now and then we catch something else. A glimpse of the future. Our future. A glimpse we caught when we came across a window suddenly flung open in front of us, its gossamer curtains lifted by a breeze redolent with the future, filling our lungs with refreshing air and our hearts with hopeful dreams.

At that window we hear something like somebody calling our name, only in a language we can't quite understand, so we don't recognize who is calling us or to where we are being called.

But we recognize the name.

Even in a foreign language, names translate closely to the original. Whoever it is calling us is calling us by our true name. Whispering to us a secret. Telling us who we are. And showing us what we will be doing with our lives if only we have the eyes to see, the ears to hear, and the faith to follow. [2]

The End of the Dance

Sometimes the uncertainty of life is scary; we don't know exactly where we're going or how our lives are going to end up. It would help to have the sheet music. It would take a lot of the stress out of life. The sheet music is what the disciples wanted when they asked, "Who of us will be the greatest in the kingdom of heaven?" Or when they said, "We have left everything to follow you! What then will there be for us?"

The bad news is, the Emperor doesn't offer us the sheet music.

The good news is, he offers us his hand.

He doesn't ask that we memorize the music or choreograph the dance. He simply asks that we place our hand in his and trust him for the next step. That is what he did with the disciples just before his ascension. Before Jesus left to be with his Father, he revealed the next step in the dance. He told the disciples not to leave Jerusalem but to wait there for the Holy Spirit (see Acts 1:1-5).

Curious where all this was leading, they asked him, "Lord, is it at this time You are restoring the kingdom to Israel?"

"It is not for you to know times or epochs which the Father has fixed by His own authority," Jesus answered. It's not important for you to know that far into the future, he seemed to be saying, but I will tell you what to expect in the next step and where that step will take you. "You will receive power when the Holy Spirit has come upon you; and you shall be My witnesses both in Jerusalem, and in all Judea and Samaria, and even to the remotest part of the earth" (Acts 1:6-8).

Only rarely does Jesus reveal the end of our individual dance. He has, however, revealed the end of the dance for all of human history. He entrusted the revelation to John, who wrote what he saw in the best words he had. The book of Revelation reads like a fairy tale, with its punishment of evildoers and reward of the righteous, with its golden streets and jeweled walls, with the banishment of darkness and the glory of the Lord illumining everything. Like a fairy tale, it seems too good to be true. And yet it is true. [3]

Bringing Them Home

The way Jesus brought justice to the world was not through loud proclamations or forceful demonstrations. He did it with the utmost gentleness. He did not fight or shout or even so much as raise his voice. When he saw people who had been battered like a bent reed, he would bind them up, not break them off. When he saw someone whose life was flickering in the wind, he wouldn't pinch his fingers together to extinguish it. Instead, he would cup his hands around the wick to revive its flame.

When Jesus came to this world, it was not in some distant ethereal display, like the aurora borealis. He came to us palpably, in flesh and blood, to live among us as one of us. He comes to us still, most often in the same way, not in some spectacular display but through the flesh and blood of other people.

We who are the body of Christ are his flesh and blood on the earth. What does that say about who we are and why we are here?

We are his eyes, so we can see people with the same compassion that Christ would see them with if he were here.

We are his ears, so we can listen with the understanding he would have.

We are his mouth, so we can speak the words he would speak.

We are his hands, so we can reach out to others the way he would if he were here—to touch them, and with our touch bring some measure of healing to their lives and some hope for the future.

That is what it means to be the body of Christ. That is who we are. And that is why we are here—to reach out and bring them safely home. [4]

Full of Grace and Truth

For by grace you have been saved through faith; and that not of yourselves, it is the gift of God; not as a result of works, that no one may boast" (Ephesians 2:8-9).

When I think of grace, I think of a figure skater spinning in the air and shaving ice on the way down. I think of Fred Astaire dancing. Of snowflakes falling. I think of Beethoven's Sixth Symphony, the *Pastoral*, especially the few sprinkling moments before the storm and the few sun-washed ones after it. I think of shade clouds parasoling by on a sultry summer afternoon. And fly-fishing in Cheeseman Canyon. I think of translucent waves curling toward a lonely sandy beach. I think of the birds of the air, the flowers of the field.

And I think of Jesus. Especially Jesus.

Full of grace and truth is how John thought of him. I think of him that way too, especially when I hear him telling the woman caught in adultery, "Neither do I condemn you. Go and sin no more." I think of him washing the disciples' feet. Of him praying on the cross, "Father, forgive them; for they know not what they do." Of him restoring Peter with the commission, "Feed my sheep." And "grace" seems the only word regal enough to drape around his shoulders.

I don't know your heart. But I know mine. And I know how desperately it needs grace. Not just to get me to heaven... but to get me through the day. [5]

A Reason to Sing

To us it has been given to sing the greatest song in all the universe.

It isn't important we sing it professionally, with great polish.

But it is important we sing it passionately, with great heart.

When we come together as Christians, united by our love for God and for our neighbor, that is when we will be in harmony with the melody of the Father's heart. And that is when our lives will become a song so beautiful it will make the entire world stop and listen.

Maybe they won't understand the words. And maybe after hearing them, they will simply return to what they were doing before. Even so, they will sense that what they have heard comes from someplace higher and farther than any of them have dared to dream. And for the briefest of moments, the heart of every last person who hears it will ache to be free.

So until Jesus returns, we sing.

Together.

In harmony.

And when at last he appears, the most passionate notes we have sung here on earth will seem only the humming of a prelude. And we will discover, some of us maybe for the first time, that the sad and sometimes somber notes of our lives were in fact the deep, visceral strains of a great, heavenly symphony.

And when we see Jesus, the One whom we have loved only from afar, we will burst into song, tears streaming down our faces, never wanting the song to end, each stanza lifting us higher to fuller expressions of love for him who sounded the first and most beautiful note that gave us all not only a reason to live...

but to sing. [6]

A Window to Eternity

C.S. Lewis told a story of an artist who was thrown into a dungeon whose only light came from a barred window high above. In the dungeon the woman gave birth to a son. As he grew, she told him about the outside world, a world of wheat fields and mountain streams and cresting emerald waves crashing on golden shores.

But the boy couldn't understand her words. So with the drawing pad and pencils she had brought with her into the dungeon, she drew him pictures. At first she thought he understood. But one day while talking with him, she realized he didn't. He thought the outside world was made up of charcoal-gray pencil lines on faded white backgrounds and concluded that the world outside the dungeon was less than the world inside.

The story is a parable, showing us that much like the artist's drawings, all we see before us are merely pencil sketches of the world beyond us. Every person is a stick-figured image of God; every place of natural beauty, a charcoal rendering of paradise; every pleasure, a flat and faded version of the joy that awaits us. But we need to be boosted to a window before we can see beyond the lines of our own experience. Only then will we see how big the trees are, how bright the flowers, how breathtaking the view.

"A work of art introduces us to emotions which we have never cherished before," said Abraham Heschel. "Great works produce rather than satisfy needs by giving the world fresh craving."

When we look at a work of art, it becomes a window hewn out of the dungeon wall that separates this world from the next. And looking out that window, our soul, as Solzhenitsyn put it, "begins to ache."

Or it should, if we are looking at it the right way. [7]

Hope Is Risen

It was in a garden ages ago that paradise was lost, and it is in a garden now that it would be regained.

But Mary Magdalene doesn't know that. For her, the hobnail boot of the Roman Empire has crushed her hope and ground it in the dirt with its iron heel.

Her hope was Jesus. He had changed her life, and she had followed him ever since he had cast seven demons out of her, freeing her from untold torment. He had given her life...a reason to live...a place in his kingdom. He had given her worth and dignity...understanding...compassion...love...and he had given her hope.

Now that hope lies at the bottom of her heart, flat and lifeless.

But something helps her survive the cruel boot. Something resilient, like a blade of grass that springs up after being stepped on.

That something is love.

Love brought Mary to his cross. And love brings her now to his grave.

But as she wends her way along that dark garden path, she stumbles upon a chilling sight. The stone has been rolled away. The tomb has been violated.

She enters the tomb—and suddenly, the woman who was once possessed with demons finds herself in the presence of angels.

One stands at the head of the stone slab; the other, at the foot. Like the ark of the covenant in the Most Holy Place of the tabernacle—cherubim on either end. For this, too, is a most holy place.

She is despondent as she tells them the reason for her tears. Then, from behind, another voice reaches out to her.

"Woman, why are you crying?"

She wheels around. Maybe the morning is foggy. Maybe tears blur her eyes. Maybe Jesus is the last person she expects to see. Whatever the reason, she doesn't recognize him. That is, until—

"Mary."

She blinks away the tears and can hardly believe her eyes.

"Master."

Overwhelmed, she throws her arms around the Lord she loves so much. She had been there when he suffered at the cross; now he is there when she is suffering. She had stood by him in his darkest hour; now he is standing by her in hers. He had seen her tears; now he is there to wipe them all away. Jesus interrupts the embrace to send her to the disciples with the good news.

"He is risen! I have seen him…I have touched him…he is alive!"

And so, too, is her hope.

What a Savior we serve—or rather, who serves us. For in his hour of greatest triumph, he doesn't shout his victory from the rooftops. He comes quietly to a woman who grieves… who desperately needs to hear his voice…see his face…and feel his embrace. [8]

A Fairy-Tale Ending

Frederick Buechner once wrote that the gospel is part tragedy, part comedy, and part fairy tale. The tragedy is that we have estranged ourselves from God, making us unlovable. The comedy is that, even so, he has invited us to the ball. The fairy tale is that not only are we invited to the ball, but we will be transformed so that we will be fit for the ball.

Transformation is a recurring theme in fairy tales. It prepares us to believe what we are promised in the Scriptures. Someday, in the twinkling of an eye, we will see Jesus face-to-face and be transformed by what we see.

Someday, with the offer of his hand, we will be welcomed to the ball.

And we will be stunning!

The once-upon-a-time magic of fairy tales that swept us away to other times and other worlds fed our imaginations, and in so doing prepared us to live by faith and expect miraculous things. Those miraculous things include the over-the-rainbow hope of heaven, the final unmasking of good and evil when each will be given its just reward, and the redemption of all creation. And all the tales of the handsome prince who comes for his one true love and lives happily ever after will be fulfilled that day, that one magical day when we see Jesus face-to-face.

On that day, the celebration will begin. There will be music and feasting and dancing. And suddenly we will realize that all our steps of following him on earth were merely dance lessons to prepare us for this one moment at the ball.

When Jesus takes our hand, he takes us places on the dance floor, sometimes to faraway, fairy-tale places. He takes us there to show us things that perhaps we couldn't see in our busy, workaday world. [9]

Joy, the Last Word

There will be a time when the groaning of creation will give way to a sigh of relief. At that time, we will share God's glory. C.S. Lewis wrote of it this way.

> The promise of glory is the promise, almost incredible and only possible by the work of Christ, that some of us, that any of us who really chooses, shall actually survive that examination, shall find approval, shall please God. To please God…to be a real ingredient in the divine happiness…to be loved by God, not merely pitied, but delighted in as an artist delights in his work or a father in a son—it seems impossible, a weight or burden of glory which our thoughts can hardly sustain. But so it is.

God's delight in us will only be the beginning of our joy. Joy is not merely the absence of agony but the presence of ecstasy. Our joy will be not only the absence of slavery to sin and corruption but the presence of a boundless freedom and the fragrant renewal of all creation. Our joy will be not only the absence of our most bitter enemy but the presence of our most beloved friend. It will be not simply the absence of darkness but the presence of God's glory that will magically illumine everything around us. It will be not only the absence of the thorns and nettles of nature's resistance but the presence of paradise, with the river of life shimmering through it and the tree of life growing out of it, with luscious and life-giving fruit hanging heavy on its branches. It will be not only the absence of death and sorrow and tears but the presence of music and dancing and feasting at the wedding celebration of Christ and his church.

It was this joy, set before him, that gave Jesus the strength to endure his cross (Hebrews 12:2).

And what will give us the strength to endure ours.

Until that time, suffering has a voice in our lives.

But though it has a voice, it does not have the last word.

The last word belongs to God.

And that word is joy!

At that word, the One we have loved for so long only from afar, we will then see face-to-face.

The beauty that is his will be ours.

So will the joy that is his.

So will the joy![10]

Finding the Center of the Universe

As incredible as it seems, there is a place over the rainbow where troubles melt like lemon drops, where the dreams that you dare to dream really do come true.

But until the day when we go to that place or the day when Jesus returns to take us there, we must live our lives *under* the rainbow...where the road ahead is not paved with yellow bricks. Sometimes it has no bricks at all, only the sharp-edged remains of our shattered dreams.

What we find under the rainbow is not an easier road to travel, but traveling mercies *for* the road, however long or hard it may be.

One of those mercies is that along the way we are given glimpses of the One we now love only from afar.

Something happens to us in those moments. A shift in focus. We find that our eyes are no longer on the steepness of the road or the sharpness of the rocks beneath our feet, but on him who has gone before us. When we see Jesus, however briefly, however indistinctly, our hearts begin to ache. In that moment and because of that moment, we love him more. And if we don't love him more, at least we long to.

It is in those moments that we discover where the Lord of the Dance has been leading us all along—into a deeper love for him.

Jesus leads us in a dance that moves around his Father's heart, in ever tighter circles, until at last we are so close to the love that is at the center of the universe that we feel it, every throbbing beat of it.

And when that happens, the beating of his heart and the beating of ours become one. [11]

A Glimpse from the Summit

The Lord is King, but for all the clouds, we can't see the far reaches of his rule. The foundations of his throne are righteousness and justice, but darkness obscures our understanding of how a sovereign God could tolerate all the wickedness and injustice that run rampant through the earth.

We may never reach a summit of understanding where suddenly everything is clear. For some cliffs are unscalable, some crevasses unbridgeable. And we may find ourselves stranded beneath an overhang, unable to climb any higher. Even if we do reach the summit, only patches of the surrounding panorama may be visible because of the clouds.

If we are someday granted the grace to sit on that summit—and it's a clear day—I think we will feel humbled by what we see. And honored. Honored to be given a glimpse of the grand sweep of God's story. Humbled to know that we have played a part in the story, however small a part and for however brief a time.

There will come a time when each and every one of us will look on our lives from the vantage point of eternity and see that our entire lifetime was just a moment to God, a mere breath. So was our suffering. Then we will look on the rewards that have been stored up for us, rewards for our faithfulness as stewards of the heavy talents of suffering that were entrusted to us. And we will be startled to see that the exchange rate of heaven is not measured out to us pound for pound because the thumb of a generous God is on those scales, weighting them in our favor. [12]

Dazzling Joy

None of us has gone to heaven. We are left largely to our imaginations to visualize what heaven is like. But we have been left with the revelations of a few people who have actually seen heaven and lived to tell about it. Isaiah was one of them (Isaiah 6). The apostle Paul was another (2 Corinthians 12:1-7). The disciple John was still another (Revelation 19–22). The revelations were so dazzling, they overwhelmed each one of them.

"Eye has not seen and ear has not heard all that God has prepared for those who love Him" (1 Corinthians 2:9). Whatever else heaven is, it is more than our experience of life here on earth, not less. It is the fullness of life, not its reduction. It is the waking, as C.S. Lewis put it, not the dream.

From the glimpses given us we know that whatever else heaven is, it is full of joy. The picture Jesus left us with is one of merriment, music, dancing, and feasting. "Enter into the joy of your master," are the words he used in a parable to describe the rewards of heaven (Matthew 25:21, 23).

Now and then we get firefly glimpses of that joy, fleeting moments that pass all understanding. Here one second, someplace else the next. With childlike excitement we follow them, hoping to catch one long enough to take in the wonder of it all.

C.S. Lewis describes the feeling as an "inconsolable longing." In those moments of longing, our joy speaks to us. It speaks to us the way the lick of the spoons speaks of birthday cake, the way the smell of roasting turkey speaks of the Thanksgiving meal, the way the scent of pine speaks of Christmas.

And what it speaks of is heaven. [13]

Notes

Material in this book is adapted from
these previously published books by Ken Gire.

Chapter 1: A Season's Silence

1. *Reflections on Your Life Journal: Discerning God's Voice in the Everyday Moments of Life* (Colorado Springs: Chariot Victor, 1998), 182-83.

2. *Windows of the Soul: Experiencing God in New Ways* (Grand Rapids: Zondervan, 1996), 16-17.

3. *Windows of the Soul*, 207-8, 211.

4. *Seeing What Is Sacred: Becoming More Spiritually Sensitive to the Everyday Moments of Life* (Nashville: Thomas Nelson, 2006), 121-23.

5. *The Divine Embrace* (Wheaton: Tyndale House, 2004), 54-55.

6. *The Weathering Grace of God: The Beauty God Brings from Life's Upheavals* (Ventura: Vine Books, 2001), 53-55.

7. *Between Heaven and Earth: Prayers and Reflections That Celebrate an Intimate God* (San Francisco: HarperSanFrancisco, 1997), 1-2.

8. *Seeing What Is Sacred*, 87-88.

9. *Seeing What Is Sacred*, 181-83.

10. *Reflections on Your Life Journal*, 56-57.

11. *Reflections on the Word Devotional: Meditating on God's Word in the Everyday Moments of Life* (Colorado Springs: Chariot Victor, 1998), 40.

12. *Reflections on Your Life Journal*, 28-29.

Chapter 2: A Season's Waiting

1. *The North Face of God: Hope for the Times When God Seems Indifferent* (Wheaton: Tyndale House, 2006), 94, 98-99, 104-5.

2. *The North Face of God*, 99, 101-2.

3. *The Divine Embrace*, 219-20.

4. *The North Face of God*, 121-22, 127.

5. *Seeing What Is Sacred*, 65-66, 71.

6. *Reflections on Your Life Journal*, 196-97.

7. *The Divine Embrace*, 207-8.

8. *The North Face of God*, 91-93.

9. *Windows of the Soul*, 156-57.

Chapter 3: A Season's Storm

1. *The North Face of God*, 16.

2. *The Weathering Grace of God*, 79-81.

3. *Windows of the Soul*, 192-95.

4. *The Weathering Grace of God*, 16-18.

5. *Seeing What Is Sacred*, 138-39.

6. *The Work of His Hands: The Agony and Ecstasy of Being Conformed to the Image of Christ* (Ventura: Vine Books, 2002), 98-101.

7. *The Weathering Grace of God*, 101-5.

8. *The Divine Embrace*, 133-34.

9. *Windows of the Soul*, 198-200.

10. *The North Face of God*, 186-87.

11. *Intimate Moments with the Savior: Learning to Love* (Grand Rapids: Zondervan, 1989), 81-83.

12. *The North Face of God*, 75-78.

Chapter 4: A Season's Promise

1. *The North Face of God*, 118-21.

2. *Reflections on the Word Devotional*, 5-7.

3. *The North Face of God*, 130-32.

4. *Seeing What Is Sacred*, 14-17.

5. *The Weathering Grace of God*, 139-40, 143.

6. *Windows of the Soul*, 216-19.

7. *Intimate Moments with the Savior*, 3-6.

8. *Reflections on the Word Devotional*, 82-83.

9. *The Weathering Grace of God*, 123-25.

10. *North Face of God*, 176-78.

11. *The Work of His Hands*, 56, 62-63.

12. *Reflections on the Movies: Hearing God in the Unlikeliest of Places* (Colorado Springs: Chariot Victor, 2000), 64-65, 68.

13. *Seeing What Is Sacred*, 4.

14. *Reflections on the Movies*, 192-97.

Chapter 5: A Season's Joy

1. *The Divine Embrace*, 60-61.

2. *Windows of the Soul*, 71-72.

3. *The Divine Embrace*, 199-200.

4. *The North Face of God*, 153-54.

5. *Reflections on the Word Devotional*, 188-89.

6. *Seeing What Is Sacred*, 192-93.

7. *Windows of the Soul*, 84.

8. *Intimate Moments with the Savior*, 130-32.

9. *The Divine Embrace*, 208-10.

10. *The Work of His Hands*, 133-35.

11. *The Divine Embrace*, 32-33.

12. *The North Face of God*, 60-61.

13. *Reflections on Your Life Journal*, 140-41.

To learn more about Harvest House books and
to read sample chapters, visit our website:

www.harvesthousepublishers.com

HARVEST HOUSE PUBLISHERS
EUGENE, OREGON